THE
MORTAL INSTRUMENTS
City of Bones

SHADOWHUNTER'S GUIDE

D1332415

THE
MORTAL INSTRUMENTS
City of Bones

SHADOWHUNTER'S GUIDE

MIMI O'CONNOR

SIMON & SCHUSTER
LONDON   NEW YORK   TORONTO   SYDNEY   NEW DELHI

SIMON AND SCHUSTER

First published in Great Britain in 2013 by Simon and Schuster UK Ltd

1st Floor, 222 Gray's Inn Road, London, WC1X 8HB

A CBS Company

Published in the USA in 2013 by Margaret K. McElderry Books,

an imprint of Simon and Schuster Children's Publishing Division, New York

A CIP catalogue record for this book is available from the British Library upon request

ISBN: 978-1-4711-1825-8

ISBN: 978-1-4711-1972-9 (Ebook)

Printed in the United States of America

2 4 6 8 10 9 7 5 3 1

CONTENTS

" There's only one thing you need to know. All the stories are true. Everything you've heard about monsters, the nightmares, the legends whispered by campfires. They're all real. Real and terrifying."

—Hodge Starkweather

WELCOME TO

NEW YORK CITY.

MORE THAN EIGHT MILLION PEOPLE LIVE AND work in this bustling metropolis, home to everyone from powerful politicians, titans of business, and glamorous TV and movie stars to broke college grads, the unscrupulous deal-makers working the dark underbelly of the black market, and the average Joe just getting by. Most New Yorkers would say they don't miss a thing—but the truth is, they miss more than they could ever imagine.

Beyond the glitz and glamour, the constant surge of commerce, and the nefarious deal-making is another world, where the stakes are much higher than anything a CEO, elected official, power-hungry crime boss, or casting agent could dream up.

There's a world far darker, more sinister, more deadly.

For those who can see just beneath the surface of most people's reality, a more dangerous, at times terrifying, New York exists, and a war is being waged on its streets—and in its landmarks, nightclubs, and homes. That charming brownstone? A demon ravaged it last night. The synagogue down the street? It's got a hidden stash of weapons to use against vampires should they get out of hand. The decrepit cathedral uptown? It houses the human race's best chance against total annihilation. And that Brooklyn courtyard? A warlock threw a bitchin' bash there the other night.

The real movers and shakers of New York are those involved in the most basic struggle of all: that between good and evil, which takes place every day under the noses of the city's denizens. The Shadowhunters—children of Nephilim, humans imbued with the blood of angels—are in one corner, while vicious and destructive demons, intent on destroying the human world, are in the other. And a myriad of dangerous beings, such as vampires, werewolves, and warlocks, keep things interesting, morally ambiguous, and sometimes dicey.

There are countless books dedicated to the subject of New York, but of course none capture the city as the Shadowhunters know it. Consider this your guide to the people and places of this alternate reality, the definitive compendium to what most people can't see in the city that never sleeps.

WHAT TO KNOW

SHADOWHUNTER

In short, demon hunter.

Several thousand years ago, demons found a way to exploit the thin veil between our world and theirs. In an attempt to save humanity, a warlock called forth an angel, Raziel of the Nephilim, who spilled his blood and the blood of humans into the Mortal Cup, from which fierce warriors drank. These warriors became the world's original Shadowhunters. The Shadowhunters are bound to protect the mortal world from demons and Downworlders.

RUNE

Ancient marking that the Shadowhunters painfully carve into their skin, which imbues the wearer of the mark with extraordinary powers. The specific power, such as speed, agility, fortitude, or clairvoyance, depends on the type of rune carved.

Placement on the body alters the effectiveness of the symbol; the closer to the heart, the more powerful it becomes.

Without runes, a Shadowhunter is extremely vulnerable.

MUNDANE

A normal, mortal human being. Anyone who lacks the sight to see beyond the normal plane of human existence. Mundanes are also referred to as "mundies."

DOWNWORLDER

Nondemon but paranormal creature belonging to a faction such as vampire, werewolf, warlock, or witch.

PEOPLE TO KNOW

CLARISSA "CLARY" FRAY

Clary is a fiery-natured, redheaded young artist who lives with her mother, Jocelyn, in Brooklyn. Clary has lived most of her life as an ordinary girl, with her best friend, Simon Lewis, always by her side. Until she meets Jace Wayland.

SIMON LEWIS

Simon and Clary have been inseparable since first grade. His devotion to her is fierce. Geeky in the very best way, he's got a quick wit and a real appreciation for the absurd.

❝ That boy is going to get his heart broken if Clary isn't careful."

—Luke Garroway

JOCELYN FRAY

Jocelyn is a painter whose talent has very clearly manifested itself in her daughter, Clary, as well. While she enjoys her craft, Jocelyn is primarily interested in Clary's well-being.

66 You think you know her. But sometimes I wonder if anyone does."

—Clary

LUKE GARROWAY

Luke is a devoted friend of Jocelyn Fray's and the closest thing to a father Clary has ever known. While Luke and Jocelyn are not officially a couple, Luke has dedicated his life to the Frays.

ERIC

Eric is one of Simon's best friends and considers himself an avant-garde New York intellectual. Clary and Simon loyally attend his band performances and poetry readings—if one can call what he writes poetry.

❝ Come, my faux juggernaut, my nefarious loins! Slather every protuberance with zeal! Turgid is my torment!"

—Eric

" You have to tell her at some point."

—Luke

" She's not ready. Not yet."

—Jocelyn

IT'S JUST ANOTHER AVERAGE DAY

for young Brooklynite artist Clary Fray—or so she thinks. Hanging at the apartment where she lives with her painter mom, Jocelyn, she's on the phone discussing the evening's plans with her best friend, Simon, and absentmindedly doodling on a sticky note. Clary's drawing a rune symbol, and when it catches Jocelyn's eye, she's quietly filled with concern.

Clary meets up with Simon for a poetry reading at their hangout, Java Jones, where their earnest friend Eric spouts some verse of questionable quality. Simon loves the time he spends with Clary; in fact, his feelings for her run deeper than friendship. Clary, however, remains oblivious to Simon's true affections but values his friendship dearly.

After a brief afternoon of poetic slaughter, Clary impulsively decides to go to a club nearby, Pandemonium. It's a vastly different scene from the coffeehouse, with edgy goth types lining up to get in. It's not the typical place that she or Simon would ever consider entering. Yet there's something drawing Clary to the club. Indeed, she finds the sign hanging over the entrance strangely compelling. . . .

❝ I wanna ask what that symbol means.”
—Clary

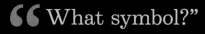

❝ What symbol?”
—Simon

PLACES TO KNOW

THE FRAY BROWNSTONE

The Brooklyn home base of Clary and Jocelyn. In the garden apartment downstairs, you'll find psychic and seeress Madame Dorothea.

JAVA JONES

Local coffeehouse, and hangout of Clary, Simon, and their "poet" friend Eric, among others.

MADAME DOROTHEA, SEERESS AND PROPHETESS

Shop of clairvoyant Madame Dorothea—located just downstairs from the Fray household—and filled to nearly bursting with occult oddities and aids for the dark arts.

GARROWAY BOOKS

Shop of Luke Garroway, offering books, oddities, and antiques with character.

PANDEMONIUM NIGHTCLUB

A trendy and intriguing New York City club frequented by various creatures of the night, both human and otherwise.

A HANDSOME TATTOOED AND PIERCED PATRON

overhears Clary asking the bouncer about the symbol on the sign and helps her and Simon make it past the velvet rope and into the club. It seems maybe this very good-looking young man and Clary have a connection.

That is, until Clary's admirer's focus switches to a knockout with long black hair and a come-hither look. As Clary looks on, the two flirt, but then suddenly the sultry looks morph into a brutal attack, and the two begin to fight. The conflict

escalates, and two men come to the woman's aid, until ultimately, one of them strikes the guy down, killing him in the middle of the club. Clary screams, but amid the loud club atmosphere, somehow no one else notices the brutal murder. The killers lock eyes with Clary. Meanwhile, the bouncer—and Simon—wonder if someone slipped something in Clary's drink. Clary is rattled by what she saw, but can't make any sense of it. She and Simon leave the club.

**❝ I swear I saw it.
There was a knife and blood.
A guy died."** —Clary

Clary sleeps off whatever it was from the night before, only to wake up surrounded by drawings of runes inexplicably done in her own hand. Freaked out, she takes off to the coffeehouse with Simon, where she sees one of the killers, a mysterious, hooded blond man, from the night before. He's watching her closely, studying.

66 I saw you kill a man." —Clary

66 That was not a man." —Jace

She confronts this stranger, and it seems he might have some answers about her drawings and what she saw at Pandemonium. But she's interrupted by a frantic call from her mother. Jocelyn's in serious trouble. She's terrified and panicking.

Clary takes off running, leaving the stranger behind. She sprints home only to find a scene of recent and massive destruction—and her mother gone. Suddenly a disgusting creature, clearly not of this earth, attacks her. Clary summons all her strength to fight it off, but she is no match for its otherworldly power. Unexpectedly, the mysterious man appears once again and vanquishes the demon, saving Clary's life.

He introduces himself as Jace Wayland.

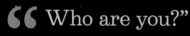 **Who are you?"**

—Jace, to Clary

THE
SHADOWHUNTERS

“ The angel poured his blood into the Cup, and those who drank from it became half angel, half human. Warriors, strong enough to restore the balance and to forever protect humanity in a war against inexplicable evil. A war that must be fought but can never be won.”

—Hodge

JACE WAYLAND

Since the death of his father when he was ten, Jace—young, hand-some, and the best Shadowhunter of his generation—has lived in the Institute with his adoptive family, the Lightwoods. Confident to the point of being arrogant, Jace has a strong moral code despite his tendency to break rules and seek adventure.

66 Jace thinks he needs to save the world. Sometimes I think he wants to die trying."

—Alec Lightwood

ISABELLE LIGHTWOOD

A Shadowhunter by trade and pedigree, Isabelle has a passion for sharp weapons, runes, and all other accoutrements of demon hunting, including her own special take on the come-hither glance. Plus, she's a virtuoso with a whip. Alec, Jace, and Isabelle form a tight-knit and lethal team. While somewhat of a Shadowhunter elitist when dealing with mundanes, at heart Isabelle is caring and loyal.

ALEC LIGHTWOOD

Alec is Isabelle's older brother and a resident of the New York Institute. However, any similarity Alec and Isabelle share in appearance, they lack in personality. Alec is very serious and uncomfortable around outsiders, while Isabelle is more of an extrovert.

HODGE STARKWEATHER

A professor of history and a former Shadowhunter, Hodge is also Alec, Jace, and Isabelle's tutor at the New York Institute. Hodge is a trusted mentor and a source of incredible wisdom regarding the Nephilim and Downworlders. Hodge hasn't left the Institute for eighteen years, but his past is filled with dangerous exploits and heroic acts.

THE SILENT BROTHERS

The Silent Brothers are an elite group of Shadowhunters dedicated to strengthening their minds through the power of runes.

BROTHER JEREMIAH

A formidable Shadowhunter solely dedicated to the study of runes, Brother Jeremiah is a Silent Brother who has mutilated his body by sewing his mouth shut and covering his body with the powerful symbols.

RUNES OF THE
SHADOWHUNTERS

BOOK OF RUNES

The Shadowhunters rely on the Book of Runes, an ancient tome, as the source for understanding these powerful symbols. This definitive guide details the runes' origins, designs, powers, and applications.

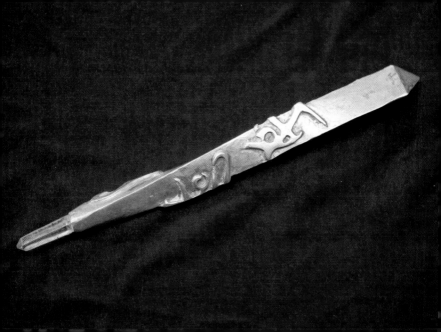

ANGELIC

Frequently applied to weapons to imbue them with angelic properties as well as wipe them clean of any demonic traces.

STRENGTH

Application of this rune increases the physical strength
of a Shadowhunter.

INSIGHT

This rune supports mental acuity
and inspired thought.

DEFLECT BLOCK

Handy in fierce conflicts, this battle rune
fends off incoming blows.

HEAL PAINLESS

Enables a Shadowhunter to heal the wound of another Shadowhunter without causing the injured person harm or distress.

SOUNDLESS

Allows a Shadowhunter to move about silently
and avoid detection.

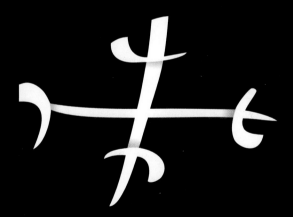

PRECISION

A modified "X marks the spot," this symbol instills in its user
extremely refined aim, typically of a weapon.

COURAGE

Provides those who wear it with bravery above
and beyond that of a typical demon killer.

SPEED

Enables the wearer to move very quickly
in any environment or condition.

AGILITY

Equips a Shadowhunter with the ability to move
deftly and with effortless grace.

FORTITUDE

Provides a warrior with unshakable resolve,
will, and inner strength.

" What the hell was that?"

—Clary

" You wouldn't believe me if I told you."

—Jace

JACE INFORMS CLARY THAT SHE HAS HAD A demon dwelling in her house, and that was what just attacked her. News like this isn't easy to take, but the past day and a half have defied explanation, so Clary seeks help from the only person she knows who might have an idea why: Madame Dorothea, the self-described "prophetess" who lives downstairs.

Dorothea gives Clary a telling tarot card reading, using a deck featuring paintings by Clary's mom. When a single card—the Ace of Cups—leaps into Clary's hand, Jace immediately recognizes the powerful image. Dorothea reveals to Clary that she's a Shadowhunter—but that word means nothing to Clary. Dorothea attempts to give Clary more insight, but the clairvoyant's powers are blocked by a spell she presumes was conjured to protect Clary. Dorothea doesn't know who or why the spell was cast. Or why Clary would need protection.

❝ There's something blocking your mind. My guess is your mom hired someone very skilled to protect you." —Madame Dorothea

❝ From what?"—Clary

❝ Your own memories."—Madame Dorothea

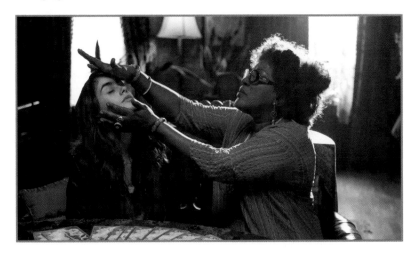

Simon arrives at the brownstone while Jace and Clary find more evidence—broken lamps, destroyed furniture, all the signs of Jocelyn's violent struggle with her attackers. Reaching out to Dorothea didn't provide

much insight, so, in search of more answers, the trio sets out for Garroway Books to talk to the Frays' close family friend Luke.

They arrive to a horrifying scene. Luke has been bound and is being viciously interrogated and beaten by two immense brutes, whom Jace identifies as two very dangerous men: Emil Pangborn and Samuel Blackwell. Using the power of the runes, Jace is able to conjure a peephole for Clary and him to peer through to discreetly

watch the events in the shop transpire. Pangborn and Blackwell are looking for Jocelyn and the Mortal Cup—the same exact object that Jace spoke of back at

Dorothea's. Luke then says things that seem to reveal his true feelings about Jocelyn and Clary, leaving Clary hurt and betrayed. A misstep causes all hell to break loose, and soon Pangborn and Blackwell are after Jace

and Clary. Jace is able to fend off the thuggish duo, and Clary, Simon, and Jace escape, but not before Jace dispatches two demon cops who had been lurking about outside with his signature scissor fight move.

Jace takes Clary to the only place he knows she'll be safe and can get help—the Institute, or Shadowhunter headquarters. To the world of "mundanes" it appears to be a crumbling, abandoned cathedral. To those who can truly see it, it's a soaring architectural beauty. With Pangborn and Blackwell in hot pursuit, Jace is forced to bring Simon, a true mundane, into the Shadowhunter headquarters. Though normally accustomed to breaking the rules, Jace is not happy to have to break this one.

At the Institute Clary meets the beautiful woman with the long black hair from the club and the other man who helped Jace kill the demon in Pandemonium. The two are Isabelle and Alec Lightwood, brother and sister Shadowhunters. What should be a moment of amazement for Clary soon takes a turn toward the

sinister: the injury Clary has sustained turns out to be no ordinary wound; she's been bitten by a Ravener, the vile demon that attacked her in her apartment, and is fading fast—very fast. Against Alec's protests, Jace uses his stele to burn a healing rune into her arm in an attempt to save her. It works, proving once and for all that Clary possesses Shadowhunter blood, as should a rune be burned into a mundane, the power of the rune would easily kill the mortal. Clary and Simon learn the powers of runes and rune tattoos, like the one now inked into her skin.

Amid the rich and exquisite surroundings of the Institute, Clary quickly gets an education about this new universe from the young Shadowhunters' mentor,

Hodge. In the relic room Isabelle similarly schools—and flirts with—a smitten Simon.

Clary learns the shocking truth of her mother's secret past as an elite Shadowhunter herself, as well as about the relic known as the Mortal Cup, now missing.

One of the three Mortal Instruments, the Cup is used to create new Shadowhunters—a race of half-human, half-angel beings dedicated to wiping out demons.

Without the Mortal Cup, the Shadowhunters will eventually become extinct; their very survival—and the survival of the human race, by proxy—depends on finding it.

WEAPONS OF THE
SHADOWHUNTERS

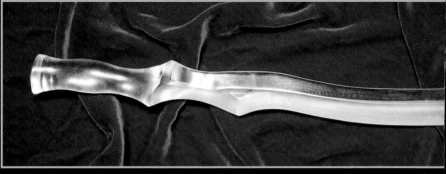

CRYSTAL SWORD

A mainstay of the Shadowhunter arsenal; capable of slicing even the nastiest demon clean in half. Used to great and deadly effect by Jace Wayland.

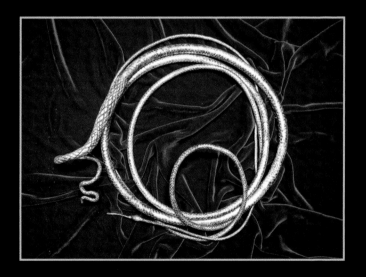

WHIP

Most often wielded with tremendous skill by Isabelle; useful when battling vampires, demons, and other assorted Downworlders.

DAGGER

Clary's dagger from the Vampire Kit. Jace gives it to her
after they mine the weapons stash hidden in the church

CAPTIVE BOLT PISTOL/ VAMPIRE GUN

Not just any firearm will kill a vampire. This one is loaded with a wooden peg—perfect for going right through a bloodsucker's heart.

INTO THE
CITY OF BONES

ONE THING IS CERTAIN: CLARY'S MIND CONTAINS vital information. Why else would someone cast a spell to block her from accessing her memories? The Shadowhunters need answers and they need them now, so they venture deep into the earth to the City of Bones to appeal to the Silent Brothers, the most feared of the Shadowhunters.

A trek to the Silent Brothers and Brother Jeremiah reveals just how much Jocelyn has kept from Clary all her life, but the spell blocking Clary's memories still proves too powerful to break. But they did receive one clue—the signature of the warlock who cast the spell is easily iden-tifiable. A visit to the one who originally cast it, the High Warlock of Brooklyn, Magnus Bane, is in order.

Magnus Bane. He lives a wild, lavish life, and the Shadowhunters decide the way to get to him is to attend one of his extravagant parties. With a little help from Isabelle, Clary is ready to hit the scene, all dolled and done up.

Upon meeting the charismatic, alluring Magnus Bane, Clary is told that the key to understanding who she is, and finding her mother, is locked within her own mind. Although it doesn't seem possible, things get even more complicated when vampires kidnap Simon. . . .

DOWNWORLDERS, DEMONS, AND VARIOUS OTHER CREATURES

"How many demons are there?"—Simon

"More than stars in the sky."—Isabelle

MAGNUS BANE, WARLOCK

Magnus Bane is the flamboyant High Warlock of Brooklyn. He enjoys entertaining and is well known for the lavish parties he throws at his loft exclusively for Downworlders. Magnus has lived for hundreds of years, and despite his party-boy lifestyle (and occasional lack of pants), he's wise and unbelievably powerful. When the chips are down, you want Magnus on your side.

66 Everyone thinks it's so great to live forever. It's not. You bury everyone you love."—Magnus

MADAME DOROTHEA, WITCH

Dorothea is the proprietor of Madame Dorothea, Seeress and Prophetess, a psychic shop in the brownstone she shares with Jocelyn and Clary Fray. While Dorothea is a bit on the antisocial side, she's also wise and a master of her trade.

❝ Did you know you have a witch living downstairs?"—Jace

VAMPIRES

Vampires, Night Children, are tricky, murderous bloodsuckers. One New York lair is based out of the old Hotel Dumont, which the vampires cleverly renamed Hotel Dumort (Hotel of Death). If one is not careful around these creatures of the night, one may end up a midnight snack.

WEREWOLVES

Werewolves are people who can shapeshift into wolves, and are sometimes referred to as Children of the Moon or lycanthropes.

RAVENER

A particularly nasty foe, the Ravener is an amoeba demon with tentacles tipped by mouths full of sharp teeth. They are shape-shifting, gravity-defying, and virtually indestructible.

ABBADON

Really big and really gross, the Abbadon is decay brought to life. Characteristics include oozing, worm-infested sores; rotting flesh; a skeletal appearance; and razorlike claws.

VARIOUS OTHER DEMONS

Garden-variety demons lurk everywhere, in the form of club patrons, mail carriers, civil servants, and even that cute little girl down the block. You'll know them by the dead look in their eyes.

PLACES NEVER
TO FORGET

THE INSTITUTE

Headquarters of the Shadowhunters in New York, the Institute is hidden behind a glamour, appearing to mundanes as a run-down cathedral. In fact, it's a majestic Gothic structure that's home to Jace, Alec, Isabelle, and their mentor, Hodge. There are several other Institutes across the globe, places of refuge for Shadow-hunters who are away from Idris, their home.

THE INSTITUTE LIBRARY

The knowledge core of the Institute, the well-appointed library is filled with tomes detailing Shadowhunter and demon history alike.

THE PORTAL

A powerful tool of Shadowhunters, the Portal allows the demon killers to transport themselves from one place to another at will, but mastering its use takes much practice.

THE GREENHOUSE

An arboretum containing a multitude of botanical
species, some known only to the Shadowhunters

THE HOTEL DUMORT

The "Hotel of Death" serves as home base for New York City's vampire population.

THE CITY OF BONES

The final resting place of all Shadowhunters.

SIMON'S ABDUCTION FORCES JACE, Clary, Alec, and Isabelle to infiltrate the vampires' lair at Hotel Dumort. It's here that Clary makes her first kill, but Alec only sees how her presence continues to put all of them in danger. Meanwhile, the bond between Clary and Jace deepens, and, after the violence at the hotel, they share a romantic evening in the Institute greenhouse on Clary's birthday.

As the spell blocking Clary's memory and abilities continues to wear off, she discovers that she possesses a unique skill, one that may help her find the Mortal Cup—and her mother. Clary, Jace, Isabelle, and Alec pay another visit to Madame Dorothea and her tarot cards, but not without consequence: They engage in a vicious battle with the demon Abbadon, and Alec is gravely injured.

The quest for the Mortal Cup has attracted the very powerful (and sinister) Valentine Morgenstern, a Shadowhunter intent on using the relic for selfish and destructive purposes. His appearance also leads to both Jace and Clary learning long-held secrets about their past that shake the very foundation of their identities.

VALENTINE MORGENSTERN

Valentine Morgenstern is a powerful Shadowhunter. Brilliant and handsome, he was once the leader of an exclusive group of warriors known as the Circle. Due to his radical agenda—wipe out all Downworlders and leave the humans of the world to die unprotected from demons—Valentine is a common enemy of Downworlders and Shadowhunters alike.

Most of the original members of the Circle have abandoned Valentine. Most, but not all.

“ Evil is a natural part of our universe. People like you, however, are evil with an agenda. That's so much worse.”—Clary

EMIL PANGBORN
AND SAMUEL BLACKWELL

The brawn to Valentine's brains, this duo of huge henchmen leaves

a wake of destruction wherever they go.

WHAT VALENTINE WANTS . . .
AND MUST NEVER GET.

THE MORTAL CUP

THE MORTAL CUP

❝ The Mortal Cup gave us hope we would live on forever. And evil would never be victorious.❞ —Hodge

The Mortal Cup is one of three magical objects—the Mortal Instruments—of the Shadowhunters. It is from the Mortal Cup that a Shadowhunter is formed.

Time is running out for Clary and the Shadowhunters. She must find her mother and the Mortal Cup first. Without it, the Shadowhunters will go extinct. And if Valentine controls it, he'll bring about the end of days.

" The whole city's changed around me." —Clary

" Everything out there is exactly the same. You're the one that's different. The truth makes you different." —Jace

" I kind of hate knowing the truth." —Clary